PRIESTHOOD: CHANGELESS AND CHANGING

Thomas Lane CM

Priesthood:
Changeless and Changing

the columba press

First published in 2005 by
the columba press
55A Spruce Avenue, Stillorgan Industrial Park,
Blackrock, Co Dublin

Cover by Bill Bolger
Origination by The Columba Press
Printed in Ireland by ColourBooks Ltd, Dublin

ISBN 1 85607 496 X

Acknowledgement
The biblical text used is the *New Revised Standard Version*, copyright © 1989, by the Division of Christian Education of the National Council of the Churches of Christ in the United States of America. Used by kind permission.

Table of Contents

Introduction   7

1. Priests and presbyters   12

2. A prophetic people   21

3. Kings, shepherds and servants   29

4. In the person of Christ   37

5. Priesthood and Spirituality   48

Introduction

In May 2003, I celebrated my golden jubilee as a Catholic priest. When I tried to re-live the years of my youth and of my seminary formation, I had memories of a very secure, self-confident church. For the most part, it was a church of unquestioned faith and order. Irish seminaries and religious houses were full to overflowing. The missionary societies of women and men were flourishing. Half a century on, all is changed, changed utterly. There have been many closures. There is a growing number of bare ruined choirs. A similar pattern seems to obtain in most of what could be called the old Catholic countries.

In the course of the half-century, a quiet, almost unnoticed Copernican revolution has been taking place in Catholic approaches to world, church and ministry. The foundations for many of these approaches were laid in the teachings of Second Vatican Council, notably in the *Constitution on the Church in the Modern World*. The popular perceptions about some of these teachings need constant refining, nuancing and even correcting. It is not always easy to draw the line between teaching and perception, between official church voice and popular understanding. The goodness of the whole of creation has been continually stressed. We have been alerted to the various forms of false dualism that can invade our thinking. The focus has been on the kingdom of God rather than on the church. We have been discouraged from facile descriptions of any one form of vocation as being higher than another. Vocation to priesthood, like the vocation to religious life, has been more and more placed in the context of baptismal vocation. The vocation to marriage has been given a good deal of prominence. While many seminaries were in their death-throes and pastoral centres were expanding, we were encouraged to pray for labourers in the harvest rather than for vocations to priesthood and religious life. In the specific context of Holy Orders, the subdiaconate ceased to be, as did tonsure and minor orders. The decision to set up the ministries of lector and acolyte had far-reaching implications. The establishing of the non-transitional diaconate and the clear teaching that deacons receive the sacrament of Holy Orders have been an important milestone in the re-shaping of ordained ministry. The new deacons are already at the service of the gospel, in church and in the market-place. We await further light on the topic of women deacons. From many sources, we have been hearing calls for a richer presence of feminine heart and hands and voices in church ministry.

It all adds up to a strange combination of certainties and question marks, of hope and of puzzlement. Each item in the emerging Catholic worldview has implications for ordained ministry. If you were to try to imagine how things will be ten or twenty years from now, you would not need any crystal ball to see that further restructuring will be called for. Worldwide, a growing number of Catholic communities are without the Sunday eucharist, the very eucharist that we say makes the church. Ageing priests are often unable to give little more than a minimal pastoral leadership. The tension between seeing lay ministry as expressing the baptismal calling and seeing it as a means of coping with a shortage of priests gives rise to a number of anomalies. The ensuing problems haven't affected Ireland in any major way yet but we are fast moving from being over-priested to wondering how we can continue to be fully eucharistic communities. In all this dying and birthing, some people tell us to await a turning of the tide. Others tell us to plan for a reverse mission from countries to which we sent many missionaries. While discernment has been going on about approaches like these, a number of new proposals have been emerging.

As we face the realities about the shortage of priests, the emphasis is sometimes placed on a re-shaping of our system as it now exists, in ways that are creative and innovative. We are invited to keep activating the priesthood to which all the baptised are called, to develop and keep building on existing church ministries, and to provide a vibrant permanent diaconate. In this setting, priests, individually and in groups, might be required to work with a number of different church communities and to concentrate on the ministry that goes directly with ordination. In communities that might be without a regular Sunday eucharist, a priority would be a high quality of the celebration of the word of God.

While programmes for this kind of re-shaping are being developed, a significant cross-section of people are wondering whether the time may have come for the college of bishops to revisit and re-formulate a question which led to a vote in the 1971 Roman synod. It concerned the possibility of ordaining people with the qualities expected of the overseer-elders described in the First Letter to Timothy. It is believed that one of the benefits of a decision in favour would be an easing of some of the tensions surrounding what, for want of better words, is described as mandatory celibacy. It might also lead us from the language of shortage to the language of new vision and new opportunity. Questions as to whether and how this approach and the re-shaping approach can be integrated require a lot of discerning, praying, and listening to the God who has many ways of calling.

We have been used to our particular Catholic tradition in which young men go away from the local community and return as ordained leaders. As one formed in that tradition, I admit that looking at some of the new possibilities calls for a lot of mental and even emotional adjustment. What is being suggested is that, as we promote the gifts of all the 'elders' in our communities, we devise a new version of the ancient practice of laying hands on some of them. This would complement rather than supplant the present system of choosing and forming candidates for ordination in the 'Western' churches that are in full communion with the See of Peter. Would it mean a partial move from a high theology and spirituality of ministerial priesthood to a more simple and down-to-earth style of priesting that seems to have obtained at some stages of the church's history? The reality is that the profile outlined for Timothy, combined with the gospel ideal and St Paul's ideal for all Christian living, could not be surpassed as a programme for any ordained leadership. Certainly the church was never more in need of a high quality of leadership, sacramental and otherwise.

Whatever our inherited attitudes or our personal preferences, we would all be at one in wishing for fully eucharistic communities in which there will be a new appreciation of our common baptism, a new flowering of the charism of celibacy and a new appreciation of the vocation to marriage. As we do all that is humanly possible for the making of such communities, we need the spirit of the workers who were asked to be like worthless slaves and to say: 'we have done only what we ought to have done' (Lk 7: 10). When we do the planting and the watering, we know that it is only God who gives the growth (1 Cor 3: 7). We keep awaiting the breathing of God's Spirit who has some of the qualities of the 'wind that blows where it chooses' (Jn 3: 8) and who keeps awakening the religious sense of all the faithful.

In 1993, I wrote a book which I called *A Priesthood in Tune*. As the quiet revolution was gaining impetus, I often thought of re-writing many of its forty chapters. Instead, I have decided to present four of the chapters as the main contents of this much smaller book. The first three of the revised chapters deal with the foundations for all ministry in the priestly people. The fourth chapter is my own distilling of the perspectives on priesthood that come from the Second Vatican Council. A new chapter is an attempt to articulate a spirituality of priesthood that I see emerging from the other four. The contents of this chapter I have been shaping and reshaping over the past few years. After a lifetime working with people in ordained ministry, my emphasis is on the sacrament of Holy Orders, and the book is intended most directly for those who are priests now. The quality of their work is crucial, at a time that is, in many senses, crucial. It is in the context of their lives that I am presenting the two final chapters. But I hope that what I have written will be of equal interest for all the baptised. In a church community that has a good priestly vision, good priests will shape a good priestly people and a good priestly people will shape good priests and help rekindle in them the gift they received through the laying on of hands (1 Tim 1:6). Priests will keep promoting the ministry of all the baptised and the lay baptised will keep helping the ordained to lead in the person of Christ. That is why most of chapters one, two, and three applies equally to all the baptised.

In a larger book, each of the topics in my Copernican list would deserve at least a whole chapter. There would be pages on the complex history of some aspects of priestly ministry, East and West. There would also be place for chapters on various suggestions for the renewal of ordained and non-ordained ministry. It seems to me that our theological and pastoral journals and the public media of communication are seeing to it that the main suggestions are receiving sufficient attention and encouraging us to explore further. Though priesthood is both changeless and changing, my emphasis is on the changeless. My wish is that this modest volume will help readers to discern which of the changing approaches to ministry are in tune with what our great High Priest would wish his pilgrim church to become, as we prepare for and await his resurrectional coming, in joyful hope.

Bibliography: I have drawn principally on the sources listed in *A Priesthood in Tune* (Columba Press, 1993) and on reports on priestly ministry from various parts of the Christian world.
Abbreviations: The standard abbreviations of the titles of the documents of the Second Vatican Council are used.

Thomas Lane CM
Maundy Thursday, 2005

CHAPTER ONE

Priests and presbyters

The English word 'priest' is a compressed form of the Greek *presbyteros*. In itself, this word has no religious connotations. Literally, it stands for somebody who is an elder, by age or by some reason of status in a community. But the word has come to have strong religious connotations. In practice, it has come to be used as the equivalent of the Latin *sacerdos*, the Greek *hiereus*, the Hebrew *kohen*. All these suggest religious, sacred, cultic functions, meanings that have been captured in the Gaelic *sagart* and related words. This ambivalence in the 'presbyteral' and 'sacerdotal' aspects of priestly ministry can be a source of confusion. It can also be a help to provide a continual and creative tension between the secular and religious aspects of the ministry of ordained priests in a rapidly changing society. It is interesting that the Second Vatican Council promulgated a decree on the ministry and life of presbyters, but its title in English is the *Decree on the Ministry and Life of Priests*. In this chapter and in the subsequent pages, the word 'priest', as applied to those ordained to serve the priestly people, will be used with its religious connotations, rather than as an equivalent of the more neutral word 'elder'.

A long history

The world has known a variety of expressions of priesthood. With their various understandings of the gods, of worship, and of sacrifice, each of the peoples that surrounded Israel contributed something to the shaping of an understanding of the priestly function. Each had had its influence on the society of the patriarchs who recognised no official priesthood and for whom the offering of sacrifice was more a family experience than a sanctuary event. In the Exodus happenings, the priesthood received a central prominence for the people of Israel. It is not easy to determine what derived directly from the initiative of Moses and what came from later developments. The end result was that the tribe of Levi, of which Moses was a member, emerged as having a special responsibility for the functions of priesthood. It is not clear whether Moses himself functioned as a priest. He certainly is presented as one responsible for the establishing and promoting of authentic sacrifice and authentic priesthood. His brother Aaron was to become a symbol of all that priesthood stood for.

The emergence of the monarchy had important implications for priesthood. In the cultures surrounding Israel, the phenomenon of priest-kings was familiar enough. Already in Gen 14:18ff there is an account of an event involving the priest-king Melchisedech, an event of which the letter to the Hebrews was to make much in describing the priestly credentials of Jesus Christ (chapter 7). The kings of Israel saw themselves as having a responsibility for the organisation of worship. Some of them are on record as having actually performed priestly functions. But the priests of the Levite tradition continued to lead worship and to consult the Lord at the various sanctuaries throughout the land, and especially at the sanctuary of Jerusalem.

Temple times

With the building of Solomon's temple, the city of Jerusalem came to be seen as the special place of special worship, of special priestly activity. In the course of time, there was conflict between the Levitical priests and the Zadokite priests who saw themselves as the official Jerusalem priests, and who controlled temple worship for several centuries. Some subtle interpretation of genealogies was needed in the various attempts to link the two priesthoods. By the reforms of Josiah in 621 BC, foundations were laid for the distinction between the priestly functions of those who were descended from Zadok and other sanctuary functions exercised by the Levites.

The Levitical priests were among those who benefited from the destruction of the temple (587 BC). In the daily worship connected with the new temple, they came to exercise a cultic monopoly and they made significant contributions to the contents of the Pentateuch in what came to be called the 'priestly' sections. The details of priestly 'hierarchy' were traced back to and ascribed to the influence of Aaron. According to this hierarchy, the pride of place went to the head priest, the high-priest, who, at least in post-exilic times, had exclusive annual access to the holy of holies, that special dwelling place of God in the re-built temple. Next in rank came the college of priests, the sons of Aaron. Next were those called Levites, with various subordinate roles. All were in various ways involved in temple worship, in the offering of temple sacrifice. Sacrifice was seen as the offering of a gift to God, in a spirit of worship and of a desire to be at-one with God. The different kinds of sacrifice captured the different tones and moods of the people's unfolding relationships with God, in their successes and their sinful failures in doing the divine will. For these failures, there was something specially sacrificial about the giving-offering of the lifeblood of a victim.

The Hellenistic and Roman influences on temple life did not substantially weaken the priestly and Levitical influence. Appointment to and deposition from the higher forms of priestly office tended to come directly from political initiative. But the basic position of priests remained secure. The high-priest especially remained a figure of exceptional prominence and power.

If one were to rely solely on the letter to the Hebrews, the function of priesthood could be seen as, in effect, confined to the offering of sacrifice: 'Every high priest chosen from among mortals is put in charge of things pertaining to God on their behalf, to offer gifts and sacrifices for sins' (Heb 5:1). This describes accurately what was perceived to be at the heart of priesthood, and the situation obtaining at the time of the writing of the Letter. But, in earlier centuries, the work of interpreting the divine will and of explaining and proclaiming the implications of the Law of God (cf Deut 33:8-10) were seen as an important part of the priestly task. As time went on, the work of interpreting the divine will tended to become more associated with the prophets; expertise in elucidating the implications of the Law went to those special teachers of Israel who were called scribes. In both developments, the growth of synagogue worship played a prominent part. The text in the Letter to the Hebrews is an accurate expression of the situation at the time of the destruction of the second temple. In spite of its restrictiveness, it captures the essence of Israelite priesthood: priestly activity was orientated towards God; it dealt with the realm of the holy; it was designed to mediate access to God; it was most characteristically expressed by offering to God, on an altar, the sacrificial blood of a victim. This blood was identified with life. Each of these expressions was to get a new meaning in the person and ministry of Jesus Christ.

The priesthood of Jesus
There is no evidence that Jesus ever described himself as a priest. His identifying with the shepherd's role and, less explicitly, with the prophetic role does not have a corresponding identification with the priestly role. Neither is there evidence that any of his hearers or immediate disciples thought of him in priestly terms. Yet if we look at what had been the characteristic activities of the priest of Israel, in the heyday of the cultic life of Israel, it is clear that they were admirably embodied in his person and ministry. His body emerged as the real temple, the only place of true worship, true sacrifice (cf Mt 12:6; Mk 14:58; Jn 2:19-21). His sole concern was to interpret and do the will of his Father and to motivate others to do that will. The words by which he interpreted and taught God's law were all life-giving words. They came from the one who was himself God's Word made flesh. He expressed perfectly in his own life the highest prophetic ideals for true sacrifice for those who offer temple worship. He is, in fact, greater than the temple, above priesthood (cf Mt 12:4ff).

When we read the gospels in this light, it is very easy to see how he soon came to be described in explicitly priestly and sacrificial terms. His death was seen by his enemies as a punishment for blasphemy (Mk 14:64). His own understanding of his coming death came to be expressed in the sacrificial terms of a body given and covenant blood poured out (Mk 14:24). With words that evoked the sacrifice that followed on the Sinai covenant, the coming death of Jesus is described as a life given in ransom by the one who is at the same time Son of Man and Suffering Servant (Mk 10:45). The timing of his death had obvious associations with the sacrificial offering of the paschal lamb (Ex 12:7, 13-22 ff). Though the sacrificial aspects of his death did not automatically make him into a priest, it became clear that he somehow wished his suffering and dying to have saving effects for others. The way was being opened for interpreting his life and death in priestly terms. In spite of his human recoiling from the prospect of his suffering, the will of his Father predominated (Mk 14:36). Nobody took his life from him; he laid it down of his own free accord (Jn 10:18). He took ownership of his 'sacrifice'. In him, priestly attitudes and priestly function were one; there was no division between who he was and what he did.

Priestly dispositions

It was these dispositions that led to his being seen as the priest offering the sacrifice that kept rising up to heaven from the temple of his own body. The fourth gospel and the other Johannine writings have various threads of priestly and sacrificial language, notably in the references to the Lamb of God. Some writers have seen priestly overtones in the account of the taking of the tunic of Jesus which was 'seamless, woven in one piece from the top' (Jn 19:23). The 'one like the Son of Man, clothed with a long robe and with a golden sash across his chest' (Rev 1:13) is clearly a high-priestly figure. The sacrificial motifs in the account of the passion in the fourth gospel are introduced by the 'priestly prayer' in chapter 17. The one who 'sanctifies' himself so that his disciples may be sanctified (v 19) is the one whom Jesus had earlier described, in sacrificial language, as having been sanctified by the Father and sent into the world (chapter 10:36). The same sacrificial motif is often taken up by St Paul. His call to a sinless way of life is based on the fact that 'our paschal lamb, Christ, has been sacrificed' (1 Cor 5:7). The day of what in English is called 'Atonement' provides him with a way of interpreting Christ's death (Rom 3:24 ff). This word brings together the nuances of expiating, reconciling and ransoming. Communion in Christ's life-giving blood is communion in sacrificial blood, the blood that redeems (1 Cor 1:16-22; Rom 5:9). By implication, it is the blood poured out in priestly action, with priestly dispositions (cf Col 1:20; Eph 1:7; 2:13).

The nearest Paul comes to describing himself as a priest is when he says that he is a 'minister *(leitourgos)* of Jesus Christ to the Gentiles in the priestly service of the gospel of God'. This priestly service of proclaiming the gospel is to ensure that the offering of the Gentiles may be acceptable, sanctified by the Holy Spirit (Rom 15:16). There is a profound understanding here of the purpose of Christian priestly ministry: letting the good news go so deep into people's hearts that their lives well lived will be the kind of sacrifice that really pleases God. A similar sacrificial perspective lies behind seeing Christian death as 'being poured out as a libation' (2 Tim 4:6). As a variation on the theme of sacrifice, some early Christian preaching and catechesis centred on the death of the sacrificed servant (Acts 3:13-26; 4:27-30). In 1 Peter, the message of redemption and the place of the blood of the lamb are expressed in the assurance that 'you were ransomed ... not with perishable things like silver and gold ... but with the precious blood of Christ, like that of a lamb without defect or blemish' (1 Pet 1:18-19).

The Letter to the Hebrews
The Letter to the Hebrews makes explicit and develops all that the other New Testament books had to say about the priesthood and sacrifice of Jesus Christ. The unknown author, writing around the time of the destruction of the temple, sees the work of Jesus Christ as, on every level, a work of perfecting, completing, fulfilling. The basic typology of the Letter derives from

what happened on the annual Day of Atonement. In the working out of that typology, all the great foundational words are
re-defined and re-situated: covenant, temple, priest, sacrifice,
holy of holies, mercy-seat. Many of the great figures and events
from the story of salvation are re-assessed in the light of what
has happened in the life, death, and glorification of Jesus. The
key to the uniqueness and superiority of Jesus Christ is the fact
that he is the first-born son and heir (chapter 1:2) through whom
God has definitively spoken. This sonship places him above all
angels (1:2), above Moses (3), above Joshua (4). As the perfect
High Priest he has the tender mercy and fidelity associated with
the God of the covenant and enriched by his own sinlessness (5:3-
27).

In his unique relationship with God, he relativises or makes
redundant all other expressions of priesthood. His eternal call
by his Father highlights the limitations of Levitical priesthood
and gives a significance to otherwise minor figures like
Melchisedech who, when seen as priest-king of 'justice and
peace', and as one who is somehow outside the normal ways of
reckoning human genealogies, provides a glimpse of what God
has done in Jesus Christ (7). With his pedigree as High Priest
fully established, Jesus has entered the holy of holies of heaven,
offering, at the divine mercy-seat, the perfect once-for-all sacrifice. Jesus is the perfect priest who offers the perfect sacrifice, the
perfect gift to God. However, he has shifted the location of
priestly ministry and sacrifice. The sacrifice is not in animal
blood but in his own life-blood. The altar of sacrifice is not in a
section of the temple, built by human hands. It is the living body
of Jesus himself (9). The reason his sacrifice fully pleases God is
that it rises up to God out of the body-temple of the one who had
no other concern than, in the spirit of the promised new
covenant, to keep doing his Father's will. In the heart of this living body-temple are written the laws of the new covenant
(10:16).

The ideal for all Christian living is to identify with the sacrifice of Jesus, in a spirit of faith and hope, a spirit anticipated in

some way by each of the well-known men and women who feature in the story of salvation (chapters 11, 12). For the Christian,
following the supreme example of Jesus, true sacrifice is a sacrifice of praise, sacrifice that continually goes up to God from the
human body, from lips that confess his name, and from hands
that shape good deeds and that are reached out in sharing
(13:15-16). It is the task of Christian leaders to keep watch, since
they must give account to God for the quality of sacrifice in the
daily lives of believers (v 17). A purpose of the meeting together
of Christians is to 'provoke one another to love and good deeds'
and to 'encourage one another' (10:24). It is a way of ensuring
that all will keep their 'eyes fixed on Jesus' who is the 'pioneer
and perfecter' of their faith (12:2).

The perfect sacrifice by the perfect priest established the new
covenant, long since promised by the prophets (9:13; cf Mt
26:28). In describing Jesus as the 'mediator' of that covenant
(chapter 9) the author of Hebrews draws on the dual meaning of
the word 'covenant'. As with the first covenant, the new one involves a whole new set of relationships. It also has the characteristics of the making of a will. It involves both a testator and those
who are beneficiaries of the will (9:16).

A priestly people

It is in relationship to the one sacrifice, the one priest, the one
covenant, the one mediator, the one will, that all language of
sacrifice and priesthood can be applied to the Christian priesthood and to Christian ministry. By calling his disciples to a life
patterned on his own, Jesus brought into existence a priestly
people, a sacrificing people. His own continual and sacrificial
giving of his life reached its peak at the Last Supper at which he
said, 'Do this' and on Calvary where he said, 'It is finished.' This
was the great act of at-one-ment. In this setting, all Christian living and dying can be seen in terms of a continual sacrifice, a continual offering, a continual libation (Phil 2:17). Even the giving
of financial support for the work of the church becomes a 'fra-
grant offering, a sacrifice acceptable and pleasing to God' (Phil

4:18). In every human situation, the offering up of the human body can become a priestly activity, bringing about 'a living sacrifice, holy and acceptable to God, which is your spiritual worship' (Rom 12:1). In tune with the godward movement of Christ's body, every activity of the living body of every Christian can be the makings of a continual sacrifice of praise. As the church of Christ came to explore the limitless implications of his call to his disciples and apostles, sacrificial and priestly language came to be applied more and more to all the members of Christ's body. This development has been fruitful to the extent to which it has helped Christians to keep their eyes fixed on Jesus (Heb 12:2), their only priest, their only mediator, of whose last will and testament they have all become beneficiaries. Whether we describe as priests or as presbyters those authorised by ordination to lead the eucharistic community, their mission is clear: to keep unfolding the riches of that will and testament and to enable every one of the priestly people to be continually enriched by the continual offering of the one acceptable sacrifice.

This is the great programme for the tripartite ministry of bishop, priest and deacon, in the one sacrament of Holy Orders. Indeed it is the programme for all men and women who minister in the name of Jesus Christ.

CHAPTER 2

A prophetic people

A prophet, as the original biblical name suggests, is one who is called and one who calls; because he is himself called by God, he calls God's people to a new way of life. A prophet is one who goes to bring an urgent message; he goes because he is sent by God. A prophet is one who speaks to God's people, not in his own name but in the name of the God who has spoken to him. The prophetic calling, the prophetic going, and the prophetic speaking have taken a great variety of forms in the course of history. As we come more and more to realise that God has always offered the divine grace and favour to every man and woman of goodwill, we have no difficulty in recognising the prophetic phenomenon outside the Judaeo-Christian tradition. In the tradition itself, prophetic elements can be recognised as far back as the religious memory can go. The events that helped the development of prophecy were the call of the patriarchs, the Exodus and the covenant, the emergence of the monarchy, the building of the first temple, the division of the kingdom, the destruction of the temple, the exile, the growing prophetic conviction of the coming of a new covenant, and the eventual emergence of that covenant.

From many backgrounds
The prophets came from a variety of backgrounds. Some were very much part of the political and religious institutions of their time. Some came from less privileged positions in society. In the northern kingdom, the prophetic emphasis was on calling the people to be faithful to the requirements of the Sinai covenant which had its own connections with the covenant made with

Abraham. In this setting, Moses emerged as the perfect exemplar of the prophetic call, the prophetic mission, the prophetic message. His call, his being sent, his message, were not of his own designing. They were the call, the being sent and the message of one who, on God's initiative, had spoken to God 'face to face' (Ex 33:11). It is in relation to that unique experience that people like his sister Miriam enjoyed the same prophetic spirit. From it came his own conviction and the conviction of the believing, hoping people that God would one day raise up the ideal prophet to whom people must listen (Deut 18:10ff). In the southern kingdom, the context is more the promises made to David and the messianic hopes that kept growing out of these promises. The two emphases did not, in fact, exclude each other. In both, the prophetic voice felt free to critique the existing approaches to law, to political and religious institutions, to moral attitudes, to ways of worshipping.

In all authentic prophecy, the prophet looked to the future and recalled the past in a way that would focus attention on what God wants from his people now, in the present. The prophets preferred to see and illumine the present rather than predict the future. A test of the true prophet was the way he could interpret accurately and throw light on current happenings and call people here and now to live the religious implications of these. In the symbolic actions characteristic of some of the prophets, people were able to recognise the power of God working through the prophetic word-actions. As the prophet held a mirror up to people's consciences, and opened their eyes to both what they were and what God wanted them to be, the prophetic word generated either comfort and consolation or anger as people saw the yawning gap between ideal and reality in their lives. The prophet either became a hero or somebody who deserved rejection, even death.

For many prophets, a test of true religion was one's attitudes to the poor. There were prophets like Amos who railed against the sheer maltreatment of the poor, symbolised in the treatment of the widow and orphan, and prophets like Zephaniah who went beyond material poverty and called for and encouraged an attitude of poverty of spirit which expressed the ideal attitude of a humble and grateful heart before a merciful God.

In these and in the many other variations on the prophetic themes, the emphasis was not on human wisdom but on the word of the living God. The true prophet was the personal recipient of that word. The word was destined to transform the prophet's own life and the lives of those who listened. How exactly the prophet received and experienced the word of God before announcing it to the people is not always easy to see. The God who always took the initiative could use any medium of human communication and experience to alert the prophet. Sometimes God had to deal with reluctant prophets, as is clear in the call of Jeremiah. Always it was his message, not the private views of the prophet, that must be communicated. The believing community helped to write down, to edit, to interpret and re-interpret the message once given.

Something entirely new
It is one thing to draw people's attention to the limitations of laws, of institutions, of moral behaviour, of ways of worshipping, and of the ways in which political leadership is exercised. It is quite another to say that the laws, the institutions and the ways of worshipping and behaving, are intrinsically inadequate and that the present system will one day have to be dismantled. This was the conviction that ultimately arose in the consciousness of some of the prophets and that came to be articulated in a variety of ways. Though prophecy concerns the present rather than the future, it is never without implications for the future. Though the prophets of Israel hoped for the salvation rather than the destruction of their people, they became more and more concerned about the state of a covenant that continued to be broken, about a people demoralised by the destruction of the temple and the ensuing exile. Even then, they remained sure that God would be faithful to his side of the covenant, and that his loving-kindness would somehow be victorious. But they became convinced that there was need of an entirely new

covenant. God would, as always, take the initiative. God still remained the loving husband of the chosen people. He would
write his law not on tablets of stone but right inside his people,
in their hearts. In the symbol of the intimate relationship of husband to wife, he would be the people's God and they would be
his people. All God's people would know him and he would remember their sin no more.

That is how Jeremiah saw it (31:31-34). Ezekiel saw the new
covenant in terms of a new heart. God would gather the exiled
people. He would sprinkle clean water on them. He would give
them a new heart and a new spirit. He would remove their heart
of stone and give them a heart of flesh. He would put his own
spirit within them and make them to observe his statutes and or-
dinances (Ezek 36:25-27). In Second-Isaiah there is the assurance
of God that he would make an everlasting covenant with the
chosen people (Is 55:3). This would be the work of the loving
husband who with 'everlasting love' has compassion for the
wife from whom he had hid his face for a while (54: 1-10).

All these and similar prophetic assurances could be looked at
as a kind of poetic exuberance but, at a time of depression and
uncertainty, which didn't cease with the return from exile, they
came to be seen by many as the strong promise of something entirely new. What precisely that new situation would entail was
not clear. What was certain was that at some stage there would
be a break in continuity. God himself would visit his people. The
day of the Lord, which in the mouths of some prophets had been
a term of judgement, came more and more to be seen as the day
when God would bring full salvation. It is not surprising that,
when Jesus came to preach the good news of the reign of God,
and when they saw that reign unfolding, those who believed in
him saw the prophetic promises as forming one pattern with all
that had been foreshadowed in the law of Moses and with the
aspirations of those who had orchestrated the best hopes of
Israel in the words of the psalms (Lk 24:44). In a sense, the whole
of the scriptures came to be seen as 'the prophetic message' (2
Pet 1:19ff) to which Jesus now was the key.

Jesus and prophecy

Jesus came to call God's people to repentance and salvation. He came because he was sent by his Father. The words that he spoke were spirit and life (Jn 6:63). He had all the best qualities of the prophets. He fulfilled the promise of God that in the last days he would raise up a special prophet, the final Moses. The coming of Jesus is presented as having been particularly welcomed by people who were shaped in a prophetic way of thinking. Zechariah saw the birth of the precursor as the fulfilment of prophecy (Lk 1:70). Simeon and Anna praised God in the same prophetic spirit (Lk 2:25ff; 36). Jesus began his public ministry under the clear influence of John who spoke and acted in the way of the prophets. He saw John as the one who put into focus all that was good in the prophets and the law (Mt 11:13).

It is clear that Jesus showed a great respect and esteem for the prophets who had gone before him. In his way of preaching, he had many of their characteristics. But he never directly called himself a prophet. His prophetic mission was but one dimension of the many-faceted mystery of the Son who alone knew the Father and who was fully known only by the Father (Mt 11:27). As his disciples saw him in action, they were quick to recognise him as a great prophet (Mt 16:14; Lk 7:16; Jn 4:19; 9:17). Jesus saw himself as at the same time sharing the worst aspects of the lot of the prophets (Mt 23:37) and being confident that this lot would, by the designs of his Father, lead to the very salvation for which the prophets hoped (Mt 21:42). But he spoke and acted as one who was greater than any of the prophets (Mt 12:41). He spoke, at the same time, with the Father's authority and with his own authority. Whatever word had been spoken in the past was superseded by his authoritative word. Without apology, he could say 'but I say to you' (Mt 5:44). He could introduce his radical teaching not with the prophetic 'thus says Yahweh' but with the definitive 'Amen, amen' (Jn 1:51; 3:3-11). Like the prophets, Jesus spoke saving words, but his words have a unique force since they come from the Word made flesh (Jn 1:14). The prophets had promised salvation. But they did not live to see that salvation. They desired to see what the disciples of Jesus saw but they did not see it (Lk 10:24). By contrast with them, the disciples of Jesus were specially blessed. They saw, in live action, the salvation for which the prophets had hoped (v 23).

Though the title prophet had the limitations of all the titles which people wished to use in connection with Jesus, it remains a very powerful key to an understanding of his person and ministry. It combines the elements of calling, sending, and announcing which were at the heart of the ministry of Jesus. It links him with all the best expectations of a people who knew that in the final stage of God's plan of salvation he would speak through the perfect prophet. It provided a starting point for the formulation of much of the church's belief and preaching. For his disciples, it illumined the events of the death and resurrection of Jesus in a way that made some of them come to see him as 'a prophet mighty in deed and word before God and all the people' (Lk 24:19). It helped them to link him with great figures like Moses, Elijah, John the Baptist and other prophets (Lk 9:8; Jn 1:25). It helped them to find a focus for all that God had promised. Above all, it helped them to see Jesus as the one to whom they should listen (Mk 9:2-9).

A prophetic church
Though, in one sense, Jesus was the last of the prophets, the gift of prophecy has always remained alive in his church. Indeed one can say that, because Jesus was a prophet, his church must always be prophetic, in a way relative to our one prophet. In the early Christian communities, in places like Corinth and Antioch, the charism of prophecy flourished. It was exercised by men and women in a variety of positions of leadership. Essentially the prophet was seen in such communities as a person of inspired insight into the meaning of the paschal mystery at a time when people very much felt the need of such insight. The prophetic person spoke in a way that showed understanding of mystery (1 Cor 13:2).

Moses, in his time, had expressed a wish 'that all the people might prophesy' (Num 11:29). In the events of Pentecost, St Peter saw the fulfilment of this wish and of the prediction of the prophet Joel that in the last days God would pour out his Spirit 'on all flesh' and that 'your sons and daughters shall prophesy' (Acts 2:17). The charism of prophecy was one expression of this Pentecostal outpouring. St Paul showed a high regard for the charism (1 Thess 5:20). Like all charisms, it exists for the good of the community (1 Cor 14:29-32). Those who use it rightly speak to other people 'for their upbuilding and encouragement and consolation' (v 3). In his vision of the body of Christ, Paul places the prophetic gift second after the gift of apostleship (1 Cor 12:28). Like all the other gifts, even these two must be lived out in the 'more excellent way', the way of love (v 32; chapter 13:1). In the exercise of leadership in the church, Paul saw a close inter-relation between apostle and prophet. The line of demarcation between the two roles would be difficult to draw. The role of apostle suggests foundation and order; the role of prophet sug-gests insight and interpretation. But the role of both apostle and prophet is foundational (Eph 2:20).

Throughout the ages, the church has remained prophetic, just as it has remained apostolic. No generation has been entirely lacking in prophetic people. The true Christian prophet experi-ences God, often at a time when many believers seem to have lost their way. He or she is generous in opening up that experi-ence to others in a way that will help them to interpret the apparent contradictions in their own experience. The prophet helps people to see that the truth, as well as the beauty, of God is ever new as well as ever ancient. The prophet shows the way for renewal and for new religious movements at times when the church is confused or at a crossroads. The prophetic insight opens up possibilities that seem to have been unnoticed. This has always been the way of prophecy.

In our own day, there have been many expressions of a yearning for a strong re-emergence of prophecy, especially where there are burning issues of justice and peace. One expres-sion of the desire for prophecy has been an appeal for the foster-

ing of what Walter Brueggemann calls the 'prophetic imagin-
ation'. Out of this gift, it is claimed, the whole of our dormant religious memory can be made come alive again; a way of living
which is an alternative to that of the dominant culture can be
made possible; new symbols can be devised to help people to
live the alternative lifestyle; people will be energised to live in a
way that is truly new and fully human; the church herself will be
alerted to her mission by voices from outside her own confines.

Priesthood and prophecy
There is an inseparable link between Christian prophecy and
Christian priesthood. All the baptised are called to be prophetic.
Christian ministerial priesthood is a priesthood of the living
word. There are good grounds for saying that the first call of the
ordained priest today is the call to be a prophet, to be a prophetic
voice and to proclaim the word of God in the prophetic way. It is
a call to live by the word and to have the insight and inspiration
to help the priestly and prophetic people to interpret their lives
in the light of the word and to be made new by the word. The
call is not confined to priests with rare charismatic gifts. It is part
of the mission of every priest.

CHAPTER 3

Kings, shepherds and servants

At first sight, it is difficult to see any connection between royalty and pastoral ministry. Yet, in the experience of the people of Israel, there was an easy association between the image of the king and the image of the shepherd. In many of the countries that were neighbours to Israel, the king saw himself in terms of a shepherd caring for a flock. Before King David was anointed king over Israel, the tribes expressed their confidence in him by recognising him as suitable to be, at the same time, king, leader, ruler, shepherd: 'It was you who led out Israel and brought it in. The Lord said to you: "It is you who shall be shepherd of my people Israel, you who shall be ruler over Israel".' (2 Sam 5:2). David, in turn, spoke of his people as sheep entrusted to his care, and he begged the Lord to save them (24:17). Having himself been taken from the sheepfolds to be shepherd of the people, he tended them 'with upright heart', and guided them 'with skilful hand' (Ps 78:70-72). The shepherd imagery was even more ex-plicitly associated with such leaders as the judges whom God had commanded to shepherd and guide his people (2 Sam 7:7), with some public rulers (Jer 3:15) and even with the princes of the nations (Jer 25:34ff; Is 44:28). At all times, though, it is the Lord himself who is the real shepherd of the people he has chosen (Ps 100:3; Mic 7:14).

Out of the experience of many good and bad forms of shep-herding, the conviction arose that there was need for a new David who alone could adequately shepherd God's people, ac-cording to the designs of God's own heart (Jer 3:15; 23:3-4). This conviction was strengthened by the growth of messianic expect-ations and by the repeated exposing by men like Jeremiah,

Ezekiel and Zephaniah of the gross neglect of the flock by leaders whose duty it was to guide and feed them. Drawing from
their experience of observing shepherds who formed so much a
part of their society, people were quick to recognise the good
qualities of the men who led them and who walked beside them
at their history's difficult stages. The qualities of the ideal shepherd were embodied in the providence and care of the Lord
himself who, when human shepherds failed, could be relied on
to feed his flock, gather the lambs in his arms, carry them in his
bosom, and gently lead the mother sheep (Is 40:11). It became
clear that every true shepherding must be modelled on, and
must draw life from, the Lord's own shepherding. The new
David, the awaited messiah, would bring together in his person
all these shepherding qualities. In some expectations, the
promised shepherd came to be identified with the one who, in
accordance with God's saving designs, would be 'pierced' (Zech
12:10) and with the mysterious suffering servant of Second
Isaiah on whom the Lord would lay the iniquity of all the sheep
who have strayed (Is 53:6).

Jesus the shepherd
Jesus lived in a society that had ambivalent attitudes towards
shepherds. On the one hand, the people had inherited all the
prophetic dissatisfaction with shepherd leaders. They were part
of a society in which to be a shepherd was to belong to a well-
known category of 'sinners'. The shepherd's way of life was believed to encourage a variety of forms of thieving and dishon-
esty. There was a particular suspicion of those hireling workers
for whom shepherding was merely a form of livelihood that did
not generate any of the ideal shepherd qualities. On the other
hand, in the light of prophetic promises about the coming of the
ideal shepherd-king, of the ideal of shepherding expressed in Ps
23, and of the people's own experience of individual honest
shepherds, the word 'shepherd' had many favourable associations and connotations as well. It may well be that Jesus was
born in a stable owned by shepherds. In that setting a group of

shepherds would understandably have been the first to welcome and recognise him. They represented, at the same time, both the lowly ones and the sinners who were to be at the centre of the ministry of Jesus.

It is easy to see that the descriptions of the mission of Jesus in shepherd imagery were drawing both on the day to day experience of the people and on the hope that had arisen out of the continual promises of God. The special mission of Jesus was to the sheep who were lost (Lk 19:10; Mt 10:6; 15:24). He was moved, with the compassion of God himself, by those who were 'harassed and helpless like sheep without a shepherd' (Mt 9:36). The God he preached was the God who is the first to rejoice at the return of the lost sheep (Lk 15:3-7). His disciple-apostles are the symbolic group that represent the coming into existence of an Israel made new. They are the 'little flock' (Lk 12:32). Through them, the whole flock is alerted to the fact that they can expect all the testings and trials that characterised the story of the original Israel, but they will be shepherded by the one who would be 'pierced', the one who at the same time serves and suffers. Out of his very piercing and suffering will come his strength to lead his people and go before them (Mt 26:31). The way they respond to the requirements of his shepherding will be the norm for the separation between those on the king's right and those on his left in his final return in glory (Mt 25:31ff).

From being experienced as the messiah-king and leader-servant who was the fulfilment of all God's promises, Jesus came to be recognised as the 'great shepherd of the sheep' (Heb 13:20). By his wounds came the healing of his flock who were led back to him as their shepherd and guardian (1 Pet 2:24-25). In the words of Moses' ideal for a shepherd, he went out before them and came in before them; he led them out and brought them in (Num 27:17). As Risen Lord, he was at the same time the sacrificial lamb and the shepherd guiding his people to the springs of the water of life (Rev 7:17). The shepherd theme is taken up very strikingly in the fourth gospel. Jesus is presented as coming to a people damaged by all the forms of bad shepherding that had been denounced by the prophets. Every promise of God to send a good shepherd and every human dream of good leadership is captured in his person and ministry. He is the good shepherd (Jn 10:11). The shepherd image captures and sums up all that his mission is about. It is about unity (v 16); it is about giving life (v 10); it is about very personal knowing and loving (vv 14, 15, 17); it is about recognising and following a voice (vv 5, 16, 27); it is about not running away (v 13); it is about the kind of love that is ready to pay any cost, even to the point of laying down one's life (vv 15, 17, 18); it is about drawing people into the very intimacy of communication between Jesus and his Father (vv 15, 30).

Pastoral ministry
Because Jesus is the only gate of entry into the life of God (v 7), and the only true shepherd, all pastoral ministry in his church must be a sharing in the mission of the one shepherd and in terms of accountability to him. Jesus is generous in admitting people into that sharing. After repeated assurances of his love, Peter is given the charge of universal shepherding by the risen Christ (Jn 21:16). One of the gifts of the Spirit for the building up of the body of Christ and bringing all its members to full stature was to be the gift of being pastors (Eph 4:11-13). The 'oversight' exercised by those called to be elders in the church is to be characterised by the full range of the qualities of the chief shepherd (1 Pet 5:1-4). The fact that the chief shepherd will come and will re-appear (v 4) is no guarantee that the flock will be spared from onslaughts by various kinds of savage wolves (Acts 20:29). But ultimate victory is assured. The human shepherd, called to be an example to the flock, can live in the full hope of winning 'the crown of glory that never fades away' (1 Pet 5:4).

Priest, prophet, shepherd-king
It is not surprising that, in the course of the centuries, the language and images connected with shepherding became very much part of the day to day life and ministry of the church. Writers like John Calvin presented the mission of Christ, sys-

tematically, under the headings of priest, prophet and king (shepherd). John Henry Newman saw the advantages of envisaging Christ's church in the same triple perspective. The Second Vatican Council fastened on this theme and taught that God sent his Son 'that he might be teacher, king and priest of all, the head of the new and universal people' (LG 13). The Council presented this threefold mission of Christ as being shared by all those who are baptised into his body. In turn, it presented all ordained ministry as deriving from the same threefold mission, and existing in order to enable the priestly, prophetic and kingly people to keep growing into the likeness of their Head. It would be difficult, indeed impossible, to draw exact lines between these three aspects of the mission of Christ, of the church, of the church's ministers. In practice, the tendency has been to link prophetic ministry with the work of preaching and teaching, kingly (pastoral) ministry with the care and concern for all the faithful at the various stages of life's journey, priestly ministry with all that concerns divine worship. This is a convenient division but, in practice, there is a continual overlapping of the three areas. The Christian minister is at the same time, a prophetic priest, a priestly shepherd, a pastoral prophet.

All works of ministry are expressions of the central Christian work of salvation and reconciliation. Each is continually calling for the pastoral work of healing, supporting, and sustaining all one's brothers and sisters, at every stage of life's journey. This arises out of the very nature of the many-membered body of Christ. Those in official public pastoral ministry are in various ways commissioned to keep promoting the call to all the members of the body to love both God and neighbour, to be the good Samaritan to anybody, anytime, in any need, to keep promoting the building up of that body which is 'joined and knit together by every ligament with which it is equipped, as each part is working properly, promoting the body's growth in building itself up in love' (Eph 4:16). The ordained shepherd is authorised to represent the members of that body to the Good Shepherd who is their Head, and to represent him to the members, especially in the moments of interaction between sacramental worship and community pastoral care.

Though the priestly, prophetic and pastoral aspects of church ministry are inseparably linked, there are some activities that particularly call for the qualities of the good shepherd. These include the various forms of pastoral visitation, care of the sick, the imprisoned, the dying, people at various stages of human 'passage', the promoting of justice and peace in the local and wider community. The church's ministry of pastoral care moves towards and flows from her liturgical life and worship, especially in the eucharist which we keep celebrating until the Lord comes. Each of the sacraments, properly celebrated, is an expression of the shepherding of the whole flock of Christ, in some way awakening and activating the pastoral urges of the whole flock, and led by those authorised to represent the whole flock. The providing for the exercise of the spiritual and corporal works of mercy, which is so much part of the church's pastoral mission, has been done in various ways at various stages of the church's history. The quality of public pastoral care has always varied considerably from particular church to particular church. One of the ways in which the church has been alerted over the centuries to various forms of human poverty and need has been the periodic emergence of charismatic leaders and founders, men and women who recognised needs and started new movements of pastoral caring. A characteristic of the whole church in recent decades has been the emphasis on adequate pastoral formation for all those in ministry. In a church that sees herself as the universal sacrament of salvation, one can hope to see the emergence of many new and creative forms of pastoral care, as all the members of the body of Christ keep interacting with each other and coming to realise that they are 'keepers' to their brothers and sisters (Gen 4:9).

Journeying together
In these times of specialisation, there is much emphasis on the development of suitable skills for those involved in various forms of pastoral care. This applies especially as pastoral care

works out its connections with specialised forms of counselling and therapy. Those in public pastoral care are learning to work in close collaboration with others who are concerned with the development of the human person. For some, this can be a difficult learning process, but for all it can be a providential opportunity enabling the church to become the kind of sacrament that she is called to be. A vision is already emerging of one human family, on one journey, in one beautiful cosmos, with one glorious destiny. St Irenaeus has told us that the glory of God is a human being fully alive, and that to be alive is to see God. The ultimate aim of all Christian pastoral ministry is to enable people to see God at every stage of life's journey, and after.

There is always a possibility that pastoral caring could generate an unconscious attitude of patronising condescension towards those to whom one ministers. The very language of sheep and shepherd is open to being misconstrued in that way. In this context, some pastoral attitudes, inherited from a less egalitarian society, are quickly seen to be inadequate today. Those in pastoral ministry need to keep realising that they are on the same journey and experiencing the same human needs and limitations as the people to whom they minister and to whom they are soul-friends. In their attitudes, they need to embody many of the paradoxes of Christianity. They need to be, at the same time, teachers and learners; walking ahead of and at the same pace as those ministered to; strong in faith yet sharing all human weakness; physicians in need of healing; leaders who are always serving; guides who are always seeking the way. This is the kind of pastoral perspective encouraged by the *Rite of Christian Initiation of Adults* which is already having such a profound influence on the life of the church. The vision it provides is of people all together on a common graced journey, walking with each other, accompanying each other, supporting each other. This vision draws continual encouragement from the exquisite example of Jesus, the wayfarer on the road to Emmaus (Lk 24:13-35): he walked with; he journeyed; he questioned; he listened and he illumined; he helped recognise; he shared.

There is much emphasis today on the human and Christian development of those in pastoral ministry and of those to whom they minister. One hopes that the church of Christ will always welcome whatever promotes this integral human development. The surest programme for the Christian side of development is being immersed in the programme for shepherding drawn up in the gospel portrait of the Good Shepherd; in the continual invitation of the one who, in a setting of love, keeps saying 'feed my lambs, feed my sheep' (Jn 21:15-17); in the daily call to be 'examples to the flock' (1 Pet 5:3). In these scriptural perspectives, there is a fully coherent programme for pastoral theology and pastoral care. It is a programme that can gracefully absorb any advances from any sources in the understanding of the human person and the skills that promote these advances. The most important requirement for anybody in pastoral ministry, and indeed in all priestly and prophetic ministry, is the ability to express the tender mercy and fidelity of the God of the covenant. The God of the covenant is identical with the shepherd whose goodness and kindness keep following people all the days of their lives (Ps 23:6). All his qualities come together in 'the great shepherd of the sheep' (Heb 13:20). This Great Shepherd is also priest, prophet, and suffering servant, the one who took the risk of being fully pierced, out of a love than which there is no greater (Jn 15:13).

Shepherding, service, ministry
The language of ministry is at a transition stage in the church today. In some usage, the word 'ministry' is reserved for those who are authorised to carry out some form of public function or office in the Christian community. Some prefer to use the word in a more generic way and to speak of the call to ministry as applying to all of the baptised. It is likely that this way of speaking will prevail. Either way, all ministry must keep trying to find its meaning and its model in the person and ministry of the Good Shepherd who was in the midst of his disciples as one who serves (Lk 22:27). In his unique way of ministering, he was, at the same time, servant, leader and exemplar.

CHAPTER 4

In the person of Christ

Ministry in the priestly, prophetic and kingly church has come to be looked at from a variety of perspectives over the centuries. If there is one key to the teaching of the Second Vatican Council on the role of the ordained priest-minister, it is attention to the fact that priests act 'in the person of Christ'. This expression comes from St Paul in 2 Cor 2:10. The context there is a delicate pastoral work of reconciliation in which Paul was involved. After a longish appeal to the Corinthian community for the forgiving of an unnamed offender, he states that he himself was forgiving him, for the community's sake, in the *persona* of Christ. In these days, in which the exact meaning of the expression is being explored, it is interesting that translators do not opt for 'in the person of'. Versions include 'in the presence', 'before', 'in the sight of' Christ; 'by Christ's authority'; 'as the representative of' Christ.

When St Jerome chose to translate Paul by the words 'in the person of Christ', the word person was already showing signs of developing a very high profile in Western theological usage, a profile that was to reach one great highpoint at the Council of Chalcedon (451), and that got many further refinements according as the Word of God in hypostatic union with a human nature came to be seen as the one subject of divine-human actions: a profile that led St Thomas Aquinas to say that a person means that which is most perfect in nature. The word that St Paul had used was the word for the human face. He had forgiven in the *prosopon* of Christ, literally before/in front of/on the side of/in the presence of, the face, the countenance, the eye of Christ.

In Greek drama, especially religious drama, the *prosopon* was

the actor's mask. The Latin *persona* had basically the same meaning. It had the extra nuance of emphasising the place of the
voice, the sound that came through the mask. The one who was
being portrayed 'sounded through', 'spoke through', 'sonated'
and 'personated' through the mask which was somehow his
face. This seems to be the most accepted explanation of the ori-
gin of the word 'person'. In passing, it is worth noting that,
though we associate the use of masks largely with bygone cultures, their proper use was, and still is, a very powerful medium
of communication. Being true to, becoming, and making present
the person we portray and represent is an admirable summary
of the call of every baptised person.

All of those baptised into the body of Christ who is priest-
prophet-king are called to be his face, his presence, his voice. In
the language of the magisterium, only those ordained as priests
are said to act in the person of Christ. Church teaching insists on
the 'essential difference' between the baptismal and ordained
expressions of priesthood, but the difference must not give the
impression of an iron wall of separation. The meeting points are
far more important than the differences, since the two are 'by
their very nature related to one another' (*LG* 10) and together
they manifest the one priesthood of our one High Priest; the can-
dles of both are lit from the one Paschal Candle and, in turn,
they help to light each other. A continual exploring of the *persona* expression can throw light on how they are related. In fact,
as we see the many ways in which the baptismal expression of
priesthood and the ordained expression of priesthood intersect,
the clearer we can become on what is distinctive about each.
Priests are ordained into a unique relationship with Christ and
with Christ's church. Though they may have other roles in the
local community, their specific ministry is indispensable. It cannot be substituted for by any other ministry. It cannot be par-
celled out to or delegated to those in other ministries. It gives a
distinctive colouring to all their activities, religious and secular.
Their leadership of the eucharistic community cannot be con-
tained within an hour.

Ordained for his face

All this is a context for seeing why the Second Vatican Council taught that priests act 'in the person of Christ'. The fullest expression of the teaching is in the *Decree on the Ministry and Life of Priests*, where it is closely linked with anointing, character and headship: 'Priests by the anointing of the Holy Spirit are signed with a special character and so are configured to Christ the priest in such a way that they are able to act in the person of Christ the Head' (par 2). In all, the expression 'in the person of Christ', or its equivalent, occurs five times in the *Constitution on the Church*, three times in *The Decree on the Ministry and Life of Priests*, and once in the *Constitution on the Liturgy*. Since the Council, the expression has had a continual, indeed a growing prominence in official church pronouncements. Pope Paul VI used it often. It has an important place in the *General Instruction of the Roman Missal* (1970), in its recently revised edition, and in the apostolic exhortation following on the 1971 Synod. It is given a key importance in the 1976 *Declaration on the Question of the Admission of Women to the Ministerial Priesthood* which was followed by the related Papal Letter in 1994. Among the many contexts in which Pope John Paul II has used it is in articulating the *Dignity of Women and the Role of the Lay Faithful*. The Congregation for the Doctrine of the Faith has been using it quite a lot since 1973. The *Code of Canon Law* uses the expression three times, notably in the nearest it comes to a definition of the sacrament of Orders (899, 2; 900, 1; 1008). It features in *The Catechism of the Catholic Church*, no 1548, and in Pope John Paul II's apostolic exhortation, *I Will Give You Shepherds*, 1992.

The decision of the bishops at the Council to use the expression 'in the person of Christ' to describe the place only of those ordained for ministerial priesthood has led to its continuing use to illumine such topics as the relationship between ordained and non-ordained ministry, the 'essential difference' between the baptismal and ordained expressions of priesthood, the ministry of women in the church. Recent study of the expression 'in the person of Christ' has shown some interesting developments over the centuries. In patristic writing generally, the church rather than the ordained minister was seen as acting 'in the person of Christ'. The shift of emphasis seems to have come with Aquinas. His use of the expressions 'in the person of Christ' and 'in the person of the church' is highly nuanced. In the celebration of the eucharist, he saw the priest as acting 'in the person of Christ' because it is here that Christ acts in a unique way through him. Similar use of the expression in describing the role of the priest is found in such writers as Albert the Great, Scotus, Bellarmine, and Suarez. The Council of Florence took up the teaching: the priest speaks in the person of Christ in effecting the eucharist. The Council of Trent did not use the expression. It was used by Cardinal de Berulle who so much influenced the French school of spirituality. A phrase like 'in the person of Christ' was used by Pope Pius XI in his encyclical on Catholic Priesthood. In *Mediator Dei*, Pope Pius XII made strong connections between the person of Jesus Christ and the person of the priestly minister.

It is clear that the Second Vatican Council was not using a new expression in teaching that priests act 'in the person of Christ'. The implication of the teaching is that a man is ordained to be a face, a presence, a voice in the name and with the authority of Jesus Christ who is always one with the Father and the Holy Spirit, and who is

- The priest who by his perfect sacrifice has gained entry to the presence of God in the heavenly holy of holies (Heb 9:24);
- The prophet who heard the Father's voice and spoke only what he heard from his Father.
- The shepherd who reveals the Father's merciful and faithful face, and knows his own and is known by them (Jn 10:14);

The ordained priest is called to promote the sharing by all the baptised in this triple mission of Christ. Though his ministry is special, it is not possessive; it is for others and it is with others. It is in the fullest sense ministerial. His ministry is special in seven ways:

In his work of unifying;

In the way he is authorised by the church;
In his relationship with the word;
In his exercise of headship;
In his exercise of pastoral charity;
In the way he represents Christ and the church;
In the way he is a living instrument of Christ the priest.

Unifying: The body of Christ on earth is the whole community of the baptised. It is to this whole body, this whole community, that Christ has passed on his mission in the form of priesthood, prophecy and kingship. The people whose ancestors produced kings and priests are themselves a royal priesthood, a holy nation (1 Peter 2: 9). The whole of the baptised people is called to be a ministering people. But in a church which has one Lord, one faith, one baptism (Eph 4:5) and which must keep moving towards the ideal 'that they may all be one' (Jn 17:21), ordination provides a sacrament of one-ness. The gift of ordination helps to disclose, make blossom, and unite the gifts of all the baptised. All Christian ministry, priestly, pastoral and prophetic, exists to reflect the face of God and in that sense must be exercised 'face to face' with people and with the God whom we hope to see face to face. This is true of the eucharist, of the celebration of every sacrament, and indeed of every act of pastoral ministry. The ordained priest brings all these 'facings' into one focus, especially when the church is most characteristically herself, in the celebration of the eucharist. As a sacramental person, he becomes one face for the myriad faces of the people who comprise the sacrament which is the church. He is ordained to be a sign and maker of unity for the local Christian community. He is also a sign of the unity that links the particular eucharistic community with the rest of the believing and celebrating church.

Authorised: Jesus in his lifetime did not answer the very important question 'by what authority?' He let the answer unfold in his deeds and in the handing on of apostolic office which was to be an integral part of his many-gifted church. By ordination, the church, in turn, through her already authorised leaders, assures her members that she is authorising and empowering the person being ordained, for the building up of the whole church. This authorising and empowering is done by the sacramental word, by the imposition of hands, by anointing and by the conferring of the 'character' of ordination (cf *PO* 2). When this character, this sealing, is seen not as a personal gift for the ordained, but as a special gift for the further enriching of the whole community of those sealed in baptism and confirmation, the priesthood exercised by the ordained and the priesthood as lived by all the baptised are recognised as flowing from the one priesthood of our one High Priest. To continue the image of per-sonating, the voices of praise from priest, people and the interceding Christ (cf Heb 7:25) together shape a 'sonata' of praise that glorifies God. The ordained priest is the 'guarantor' for the community of the baptised that each eucharistic celebration is an authentic 'appearing' of the crucified and risen Lord who has 'entered into heaven itself, now to appear in the presence of God on our behalf' (Heb 9:24). This is the significance of the fact that, in the list of the ways in which Christ is present in the sacrifice of the Mass (*SC* 3), a special presence is linked with the person of the priest-minister. This presence is for the gathering and lifting up of the gifts of all the members of the body and the guaranteeing that the sacrifice which Christ offered once-for-all for his close disciples and for all is being made sacramentally present in this particular memorial, in this particular sacred banquet. At all times the ordained person exercises his authority in communion with the rest of the presbyterate and with the bishop who has the fulness of the sacrament of Holy Orders and is the sign of unity for this particular diocesan church.

The word: There have been many attempts to answer the question 'What is the theological starting point for a definition of the priestly ministry?' Some like to start with pastoral leadership. Some start with the preaching of the word of God. Some start with the celebration of the eucharist. The three are, in fact, inseparable. What unifies all three is seeing priestly ministry in terms of a relationship with the Word of God and with the proclaiming of his word. This was put very effectively by Karl

Rahner when he stated that 'the priest is he who, related to an at least potential community, preaches the word of God by mandate of the church as a whole and therefore officially, and in such a way that he is entrusted with the highest levels of sacramental intensity of this word ... (*Concilium* Vol 3, No 5). The priest's special relationship with the word must never be isolated from his community leadership, liturgical and pastoral. This is why Rahner was careful to emphasise that 'the proclaiming of the word and the administering of the sacraments have therefore a common root and are ultimately one in nature'. Pastoral ministry, in turn, is the bringing of the word of God into every human situation. Pastoral leadership is a function of the word. The preached word, the word proclaimed in sacrament, and the pastoral word, are one. In all three the 'flock of God' are 'fed' by the one word (cf 1 Pet 5: 2).

Headship: When the word of God is proclaimed at its highest level of sacramental intensity, especially in the sacraments of eucharist and reconciliation, the priest exercises a unique sharing of Christ's headship of the church. In the eucharist, he is presiding at the celebration which is the summit and source of the whole church's existence (*SC* 10). In the sacrament of reconciliation, he is speaking words which are the high sacramental point of a process that should be continually going on in multiple forms in all the Christian community and in the wider society which the church serves. In both, the headship of the ordained person is the sacramental assurance of the saving presence of Christ to all the members of his body. This is why the fuller description of priesthood in the teaching of the Second Vatican Council is in terms of acting in the person of Christ 'the Head' (*PO* 2). This headship and leadership is not confined to sacramental activity. It overflows into every expression of pastoral care, by those called to be 'examples to the flock' (1 Pet 5: 3). Those ordained to priesthood act in the person of Christ who is at the same time Head and Shepherd. They are 'a sacramental representation of Jesus Christ, the Head and Shepherd' (*I Will Give You Shepherds,* par 15). In the biblical imagery, the head expresses authority, but, at the same time and inseparably, it expresses the giving of life and the encouraging of life.

The headship of Christ is never a headship of domination or mastery since Christian power is the exact opposite of worldly power. The only headship which Christ recognises as exercised in his name is a headship of love, a headship of self-giving, a headship of self-sacrifice, a headship of service, a headship in which the Head is in continual life-giving organic interaction with all the members of the body, all of whom share his priestly, prophetic and kingly mission. It is a sharing in the headship of the one who 'loved the church and gave himself up for her ... that she may be holy and without blemish' (Eph 5: 25-27). It is a sharing in the headship of the one who taught 'with you ... this must not happen. No, the greatest among you must behave as if he were the youngest, the leader as if he were the one who serves ...' (Lk 22: 24-27). It is a headship which glories only in the cross of our Lord Jesus Christ. Any day on which ministerial priesthood is perceived as domination or monopoly is a day on which what should be light has been turned into darkness. It is for the same reason that the ordained person should see no threat in sharing many of the elements of 'in the person of Christ' with the rest of the baptised. The fact that, in official church usage, the expression is applied only to the ordained is a continual reminder of that 'head-ship' and unique relationship to the word that is proper to those exercising ordained pastoral leadership.

Pastoral charity: In the continual cycle of ministries in which the preached word leads up to its highest level of sacramental intensity and out to pastoral care and back again to sacrament, the priest must be truly a man of face, a face that reflects the heart and voice of the Good Shepherd. It is in line with this vision that the Second Vatican Council spoke about the quality of pastoral charity that flows from ordained leadership (*PO* 16). Pastoral charity is the fruit of the mutual love between the ordained person and the Good Shepherd whose charity he helps to mediate. In the man of true pastoral charity, word, sacrament and pastoral headship become one and they authenticate each other. This is the ministry of unifying, in action. Sunday celebration will be unreal without weekday pastoral concern; the real meaning and purpose of pastoral concern will be unfolded on Sunday.

All this will show in the face of one who is always strongly present to the Christian community, and who is not just one who puts in appearances. True to the mystery of the Incarnation, his ministry will always be 'embodied' in the day to day realities of the lives of people he anoints in a variety of ways. The details as to how pastoral charity and pastoral unifying are to relate to and overflow into and intersect with educational, economical, political and social interests will vary in different human situations, in different cultures.

Representing: All priestly ministry, whether baptismal or ordained, is an exercise in presence. In the sacramental life of the church, every aspect of the mystery of Christ is continually being made present. One expression of presence is re-presenting. A man is ordained to represent Christ and to represent the Christian community. Does he directly represent Christ, or does he directly represent the priestly people, and through them represent Christ, the Head of the body, thus acting 'in the person of the church?' It has always been a strong conviction of the Christian churches that it is the risen Lord himself who, through his Spirit, calls and commissions for ministry. In this context, one must say that the ordained person directly represents Christ, the living and life-giving Head of his body the church. But from the perspective of Christ's handing over his whole mission to his whole body, and bearing in mind the inseparable union between Head, members and minister, the second approach has many attractive elements. The ordained person's ministry finds its meaning only in the heart of the people whose faith, devotion and worship he represents, and in whose name he presides. The priest's unique way of imaging Christ is by representing Christ the Head to the members of the living body, all of whom themselves represent and image Christ in unique and irreplaceable ways.

Representing is a key word in contemporary approaches to ordained priesthood, as it has been in various ways in the past. As well as being prominent in Catholic thought, it has an important place in the ARCIC and Lima ecumenical statements. The priest represents Christ who is the one Head of the whole mission-filled body. This re-presenting means that he is an effective sign of the continual active presence of Christ, the Head, to the members of his body. He is sacramentally authorised to represent Christ, the 'sacrament' of God's saving work, in the middle of the church which is Christ's sacrament. There are times, even in the eucharist, when his words are in the form of reported speech. In addressing the Father about the work accomplished by his Son, he speaks of the Son in the third person: 'He took bread ... he blessed ...' But what is special to his sacramental role is that he speaks in the name and person of Christ, the Head of the body of the faithful, in the celebration in which Head and body are uniquely united. He is both related to the Head through the church and through the Head to the church. The ideal is that his ministry in the person of Christ the Head and his ministry in the person of the church should form a harmonious unity.

Instrument: Over seven centuries ago, St Thomas described ordained priesthood in terms of instrumental causality. In these days of the primacy of persons, the language of instruments may seem strange and arid. But there is a perennial appeal in the image of the good musician playing on a well-tuned instrument and in the thought of what an instrument can become in the hands of a master-craftsman. Nobody has written more sensitively about what human instruments can become than did Aquinas. In the eucharist especially, he saw the whole priestly people as raised to a special level of instrumentality. In this setting, he pointed out the necessity that there be only one minister who is specially empowered by God to represent Christ. His understanding of instrumentality is closely linked with his understanding of sacramental character and its place in the special participation of the ordained person in the priesthood of Christ.

In that participation, every one of the priest's human qualities and talents can become a living instrument of salvation.

The language of instrumentality continues to be used in official church teaching. For the ordained person, it is a salutary reminder to keep looking to the One in whose hands he is an instrument and to keep renewing his desire to be a willing and loving agent of the church's one Head.

In-personating

Does the language of 'in the person of Christ', *in persona Christi*, suggest acting a part and impersonation? As always, we are dealing here with the limitations of all human language and imagery. There certainly is an ambivalence in the mask image, in particular. The man who wears a mask or *persona* can become a caricature or a phantom person. A *persona* can conceal and distort, as well as reveal. The suggestion of 'masked men' can have hideous connotations. The hardest thing Jesus said about the Pharisees was that they were 'hypocrites', literally stage actors, masked men. But being *in persona* is a programme and a life-long process. All through his life, the ordained person is invited to grow into the *persona* of Christ, grow up into the Head (Eph 4: 15). Instead of seeing him as 'impersonating' Christ, perhaps we should say that he is called to a daily conversion that will enable him to be an authentic image, 'in-personating' Christ. In this, he is beyond acting; he is exercising a ministry of transparency.

CHAPTER 5

Priesthood and Spirituality

I am not a diocesan priest. I am not a religious. As a member of what in Canon Law is called a society of apostolic life, I recognise my countless affinities with priests who celebrate the sacred in the midst of the secular. I like to believe that the Vincentian colouring of my spirituality keeps me in touch with their way of life and helps me to be part of their brotherhood. More and more, I am seeing the priestly ministry of all of us in terms of our relationship with the living word of the Word made flesh. We were all ordained to proclaim the word of God, to celebrate the word of God in its unique sacramental intensity in the eucharistic sacrifice, and to shepherd people by bringing the saving word into every area of human living.

I cannot forget the final session of a workshop in which I once gave two inputs on the centrality of the word of God in priestly ministry. A priest stood up and said that I had given a good description of the vocation of a monk but that I hadn't really touched into his own life as a diocesan priest. To put it mildly, I was taken aback. Nearly twenty years on, his comments are still rankling, somewhat. I was reminded of them a few years ago when the *Glenstal Book of Prayer* got such an enthusiastic reception. It is clear that, from the monastic matrix, thousands of lay people, priests and members of apostolic religious communities are getting a new vision of the possibilities of prayer in their daily lives. For me, it is one more indication that the day to day responding to the word of God, the continual signing of oneself in the name of the Trinity, the devout calling on the names of Jesus, Mary and Joseph, the living of the whole Sermon on the Mount and of the whole Paschal Mystery, the responding in faith, hope and love to each item of the Creed, from 'I believe in one God' to 'the resiurrection of the body and life everlasting', are incomparably more important than any applied expression of Christian spirituality.

My search for a word

For some time past, I have been searching for a word that can make this one Christian spirituality take flesh in the whole spectrum of lifestyles, from desert and monastery to family and market-place, from lay call to ordained call. The word that now satisfies me most is 'particular'. I continue to be intrigued by the way the *Decree on the Pastoral Office of Bishops* spoke of the 'particular church'. The particular church comprises this group of believers and worshippers at this particular time, with these particular testings, with this particular tradition, with the leadership of this particular presbyterate, and the unifying influence of this particular bishop. From reflecting on this way of seeing the Church, I have come to think in terms of universal Christian spirituality and particular Christian spirituality. Every man, woman and child is a person of many particularities. These cannot be developed in isolation. If I keep opening myself to the whole Christian tradition, to the experience of people of other religions and to the human experience generally, my spirituality can become very much enhanced. If I become preoccupied with my own particularities, I might end up with a glow-worm spirituality.

We have, sadly, been hearing a lot about scandals. In the middle of the nineteenth century, Soren Kierkegaard talked about a different kind of scandal. He called it the scandal of particularity. For him, the scandal was in the fact that God should choose to reveal the divine secrets through a particular, undistinguished people, in a particular culture, throughout a particular span of history. All these bear obvious marks of limitation, weakness and imperfection. Kierkegaard himself made the most of this scandal of particularity. His strongest contribution to the promotion of Christian attitudes was in his beaming the gospel ideal on to the individual and particular situations in which people find themselves. He helps us to remember that, scandal or no scandal, the God we worship is the God of particularities. In the language of Ps.139, God searches each one of us and knows us; God knit each of us together; all the days of each of us are written in God's book. God calls each of us to live the Creed and to practise the commandment of love with our particular temperament, with our particular story, and in the particular set of circumstances that are uniquely our own.

It wasn't part of God's plan that I should live a life of faith, hope and pastoral charity at any of the allegedly more secure times in the Church's history. Neither will I be called to do so in the changed and possibly more humanly satisfying times of the future. As a fisher for people, I keep letting down the nets to reach whatever is in this water now. My call comes only at this particular time, in close collaboration with this particular group of men and women, in ordained and non-ordained ministry. The directive in the *General Instruction on the Roman Missal* (1970) and in its recently revised edition (No 18) that, in organising the details of each eucharistic celebration, the particular character and circumstances of the present assembly must be taken into account has implications for every aspect of our theology, every aspect of our liturgy, every aspect of our spirituality, every aspect of our daily living, every aspect of the many ways we are called to be eucharistic. In days gone by, we introduced the Gospel of the day with 'at that time, Jesus said to his disciples'. I sometimes feel the urge to replace these words with 'at this time, Jesus is saying to us his disciples'

Many calls; one call

So how would I name the parameters within which I can best understand the particular spirituality that should pervade my day-to-day life as a priest, as my spirit keeps recognising and responding to the Spirit of Christ? I like to list them not as a complicated unattainable programme but as seven ways in which I can be and recognise the face of Christ in any ordinary day:

- As an ordained disciple, I am called *to follow Jesus Christ*, step by step, in all my moments of sorrow, joy, glory, light. My particular call as a priest-discile is in terms of the person and face of Christ. The face of Christ reveals the face of the Father who keeps on sending the Spirit of his Son into our hearts. This is why I am called to a daily ministry of fathering and spiriting, in a way that is best expressed as I lead the sacrifice-memorial-meal that is the eucharist. In one of the eucharistic prayers, I ask the Father to fill the eucharistic community with his Holy Spirit so that they will become one body, one spirit in Christ. I go on to pray that the Holy Spirit will make us an everlasting gift to the Father and enable us to share in the inheritance of the saints. All spirituality of priesthood is somehow enfolded here.

- As I follow Jesus Christ who humbled himself to share in our humanity, I am called to be *more human* and to promote whatever is good for health of body, mind and spirit in myself and in others. Thomas Merton who himself, in so many ways, drank the cup of human sadness as well as the cup of human gladness, used to tell his novices that to become saints they must first become men. In my journey to becoming human, I need continual patience with the workings of my body, in its interaction with my mind and spirit. As I learn more about my chemistry, my genes, my hormones and my flowing adrenalin, I can see why, in programmes for priestly formation today, there is so much emphasis on human formation. Maybe it was to my blindness regarding this aspect of spirituality that the priest was pointing two decades ago.
  In my own fragility and in my identifying with human weakness, I manifest the broken but beautiful face of Christ.

- I am called to be a *lover*. Jesus was totally unambiguous about what constitutes the greatest commandment. It is a call to the kind of love that absorbs all one's heart, soul and might. In this setting, the celibate way of life, though it is a treasure in a very earthen vessel, can keep contributing to genuine human growth. At a time of much questioning about the links between celibacy and diocesan priesthood, I need to remember that the celibate lifestyle is a privileged way of following Jesus Christ whose zeal for the coming of his Father's reign left him no space for becoming a husband or father. It is into this way that I have vowed myself. It is into this way of gospel living and loving that my diocesan neighbours were ordained. My desire to grow in this gospel way keeps getting new energy from my reflecting on the life of my Lord who came to bring fire to the earth. The accounts of his testings indicate that his life was the continual expression, at any cost, of an undivided heart, of a readiness to keep pouring out his soul as a ransom for many, of a continual renouncing of what the world regarded as might, in a way that involved continual self-emptying. The particularities of my priestly call to love are in the many opportunities for pastoral charity, as I try to help any brother or sister who is in any form of human need and as I try to speak the prophetic word of God into their lives, with or without words, and whatever their belief or unbelief, their language or their colour.

- I am called to be *a man of blessings*. Blessing others is not the monopoly of the ordained. Fathers and mothers are called to bless their children. All believers are called to bless each other, in sickness and in health. The blessing that is given by an ordained person and the blessings he encourages people to give each other are continually re-sourced from the eucharistic words which he daily says in the person of Christ: 'He took, he blessed, he broke, he gave'. 'Blessing' God who is the source of all blessings overflows into blessing people. Priests are further asked to bless the great diversity of things that form part of the daily interaction of people with each other and with the rest of creation. Hence the Church's books of blessings. The sensitive use of these blessings helps me as a priest to promote a healthy appreciation of the sacramentals which are in so many ways related to the sacraments. A test of this sensitivity is my choice of and placing of crucifixes, images and statues, in the church, in church-related buildings, and in the space in which I live.

- I am called to be *a man of the book*. In a sense, the only book for Christians is Jesus Christ, the letter the Father has written us from heaven. But there is a book written on earth that puts us in touch with God in a special way. In recent years we have been seeing ever more clearly that all our specialised books, of rules, of constitutions, of spiritualities, must be read and prayed in the perspective of that privileged book. Significantly, its very name is the *biblion*, the Bible, the book. As a priest, I have other books that throw light on and are lit up by that special book. These are the *Lectionary*, the *Sacramentary*, the *Prayer of the Church*, and the various ritual books used in the celebration of the sacraments and blessings. It is out of these books that the spirituality of a priest is specially minted. The particularities in my use of them comes from my being sent as a leader in the Church's sacramental and pastoral life. The *Prayer of the Church* is not the special monopoly of the ordained. As a priest, I pray with and in the name of the believing and praying Church. I am encouraged to pray in a way that provides continual nourishment for myself and for the whole community of believers. In the growing popularity of practices like *Lectio Divina*, I am finding more and more opportunities for this work of nourishing.

- I am called to communicate daily with my Lord in *face to face prayer*, for the time and in the place and space that are most conducive to let heart speak to heart. This time, this place, this space will be subject to some day-to-day variations, the particularities of which I alone can decide. Even with the best of planning, many of my days will be 'pieces and patches, without any stitches'. There will be many days when tiredness or a succession of apparently trivial calls will make many inroads into the flow of my prayer. There will be days in which there won't even be the beginnings of a flow. I keep learning what happens to the best made plans. I take heart from St. Vincent de Paul's reminder that there are times when we must leave God for God.

   But no fragmentation should be allowed take from my basic desire to sustain a heart-to-heart communication with the Lord before whose face I am called to live and whose face I am called to be. This communication is my response to the same Lord's invitation to pray always. My personal prayer tunes me into the prayer of the woman who is mother of my Lord and of his Church, and the prayer that keeps rising up from the whole communion of saints. Being fully alive in the communion of saints will help me to communicate, to have a sense of community, to be eager to collaborate and to resist every temptation to be a lone ranger as the ministry of the future takes shape. One of the particularities of my personal prayer as a priest is that I come with all the needs of the community of which I am a servant and many of whom keep asking me to pray for them. They will somehow feature in my examen at the end of the day. I like to think that when Jesus spent whole nights in the prayer of the Father he brought with him the needs of the people who had come to him in the day that had just ended.

- I am called to a daily *change of heart*, a daily conversion.

This change of heart is very closely connected with my ministry of forgiveness and reconciliation. My effectiveness as an agent of reconciliation, as I tune in to the real hurts and divisions in the particular community which I am serving, will be very much strengthened by the way I myself receive the sacrament of reconciliation, and the way I humbly seek pardon from the people I have offended and keep offending.

A saint of the particular

I have been trying to articulate a spirituality that one might call the sacrament of the particular. As a patron for a spirituality of the particular, none of us could do better than choose the new doctor of the Church, St. Thérèse. She chose all. She wished to follow every calling, to be a martyr, a warrior, a priest…She got all these into focus by wishing to be love in the heart of the Church. She said she wished to love Jesus with a passion and to give him a thousand proofs of her love. The daily thousand proofs were not just a cosy ideal. They were concretised in a particular community, towards a particular prioress, towards particular sisters, in prayer for two particular priests, in the performance of particular religious and other exercises. It is in these particularities, each with its own group of human limitations and frustrations, that she achieved her great ambition to choose all and be love in the heart of the Church. She continues to send out new currents of that same love.

Epilogue

Just a week after my golden jubilee and my seventy-fifth birthday, I began to listen, as if for the first time, to the story of Abraham, the father of believers. For several days, it provided the first reading in the daily eucharist. It struck me forcibly that it is a splendid backdrop for understanding the Church's pilgrim journey today. I was encouraged by the reminder that Abraham was seventy-five years old when his big mission began (Gen 12: 4). I heard him being told to go out into an unfamiliar land that the Lord would show him (v 1). I listened to the assurance that God would bless him, that he would be a blessing, and that in him all the nations would bless themselves (vv 2, 3). I was impressed by the account of the hospitality of Abraham and Sarah (18: 1ff) which would one day provide the inspiration for a great icon on the Trinity. I was moved by Abraham's readiness to make the great sacrifice as he said 'Here I am' (22: 1ff). It reminded me of the *adsum* I said at ordination and the 'present' which candidates say today as they promise to keep really present to the Lord who, in so many ways, is always really present in his Church. I got new hope from the account of the way God gave fertility where Abraham and Sarah experienced only barrenness (18: 10ff).

I began to see more clearly why the daily *Prayer of the Church* begins with the covenant-oath that God swore to Abraham and moves into evening by joining Mary as she magnifies the Lord for his mercy to Abraham and his descendants forever. I could understand why the Letter to the Hebrews presents Abraham as a model of faith and hope (Ch.11) and lists him in the great cloud of witnesses that keep cheering us on (Ch.12). The same Letter presents him as a model for all those who have to set out not knowing where they are going (Ch.11: 9). It is with this programme of pilgrim faith and hope that the unknown author invites us to let mutual love continue (Ch.13: 5). A very suitable model and a very suitable programme for a priesthood that is both changeless and changing!